Contents

Appetizers & Snacks 2

Soup's On 12

30-Minute Dishes 22

Family Favorites 34

Holiday Fun 44

Vegetables and Sides 56

Sweet Treats 68

Beverages 84

Index 95

Appetizers & Snacks

Italiano Fondue

START TO FINISH: 20 minutes

Prepping: 5 minutes
Cooking: 10 minutes
Standing: 5 minutes

- 1¾ cups Prego® Traditional Pasta Sauce
- ¼ cup dry red wine
- 1 cup shredded mozzarella cheese (4 ounces)

Suggested Dippers: Warm Pepperidge Farm® Garlic Bread, cut into cubes, meatballs, sliced cooked Italian pork sausage, breaded mozzarella sticks **and/or** whole mushrooms

1. Mix the pasta sauce and wine in a 1-quart saucepan. Bring to a boil over medium heat, stirring often. Cook for 5 minutes for the alcohol to evaporate.

2. Pour the sauce into a fondue pot or slow cooker. Stir in the cheese. Let stand for 5 minutes for cheese to melt slightly.

3. Serve warm with *Suggested Dippers*.

Makes: 2 cups

Layered Pizza Dip

START TO FINISH: 30 minutes

Prepping: 10 minutes
Baking: 15 minutes
Cooling: 5 minutes

- 1 cup part-skim ricotta cheese
- ½ cup chopped pepperoni
- 1 cup shredded mozzarella cheese (4 ounces)
- 1 cup Prego® Pasta Sauce, any variety

Pepperidge Farm® Garlic Bread, any variety, heated according to package directions **or** Pepperidge Farm® Crackers, any variety

1. Spread the ricotta cheese in an even layer in a 9-inch pie plate. Top with ¼ **cup** of the pepperoni and ½ **cup** mozzarella cheese. Carefully spread the pasta sauce over the cheese. Sprinkle with the remaining pepperoni and mozzarella cheese.

2. Bake at 375°F. for 15 minutes or until hot. Let cool for 5 minutes.

3. Serve with the garlic bread or crackers for dipping.

Makes: About 3 cups

Easy Substitution Tip: Substitute or add any of the following toppings for the pepperoni: Sliced pitted olives, sliced mushrooms, chopped sweet peppers **or** chopped onions.

Appetizers & Snacks

Walnut-Cheddar Ball

START TO FINISH: 2 hours 20 minutes

Prepping: 20 minutes
Refrigerating: 2 hours

- 2 cups shredded Cheddar cheese (8 ounces)
- ½ cup finely chopped walnuts
- ¼ cup mayonnaise
- 1 medium green onion, chopped (about 2 tablespoons)
- 1 tablespoon Dijon-style mustard
- 1 teaspoon Worcestershire sauce
- ¼ cup chopped fresh parsley
- 1 tablespoon paprika

Pepperidge Farm® Cracker Quartet or Cracker Trio Entertaining Collection Cracker Assortment

1. Mix the cheese, walnuts, mayonnaise, green onion, mustard and Worcestershire in a 1½-quart bowl.

2. Mix the parsley and paprika on a piece of wax paper. Shape the cheese mixture into a ball, then roll in the parsley mixture to coat. Wrap in plastic wrap. Refrigerate for 2 hours or until firm.

3. Unwrap the cheese ball and place on a serving plate. Serve with the crackers.

Makes: 2 cups

Appetizers & Snacks

Tex-Mex Toasts

START TO FINISH: 22 minutes

Prepping: 20 minutes
Baking: 2 minutes

- 1 package (9.5 ounces) Pepperidge Farm® Mozzarella & Monterey Jack Cheese Texas Toast
- 6 tablespoons Pace® Refried Beans
- Pace® Chunky Salsa, any variety
- Sour cream (optional)
- Chopped green onions (optional)

1. Prepare the toast according to the package directions.

2. Spread **1 tablespoon** of the beans on each toast slice. Bake for 2 minutes more or until hot.

3. Top each toast slice with salsa, sour cream and green onions, if desired.

Makes: 6 servings

Cooking for a Crowd: Recipe may be doubled.

Appetizers & Snacks

Spicy Grilled Quesadillas

START TO FINISH: 17 minutes

Prepping: 10 minutes
Grilling: 5 minutes
Standing: 2 minutes

- 8 flour tortillas (8-inch)
- 2 cups shredded Cheddar cheese (8 ounces)
- 1 jar (16 ounces) Pace® Chunky Salsa, any variety
- 1 cup diced cooked chicken
- 4 medium green onions, chopped (about ½ cup)
- Vegetable oil
- 1 cup sour cream

1. Put **4** of the tortillas on a work surface. Top each with **½ cup** of the cheese, **¼ cup** salsa, **¼ cup** chicken and **2 tablespoons** green onions. Top with the remaining tortillas.

2. Lightly oil the grill rack and heat the grill to medium. Brush the tops of the quesadillas with some oil. Place the quesadillas oil-side down on the grill for 3 minutes. Brush the tops of the quesadillas with some oil and turn over. Grill for 2 minutes more or until lightly browned. Remove the quesadillas from the grill and let stand for 2 minutes.

3. Cut the quesadillas into wedges. Serve with the remaining salsa and sour cream.

Makes: 4 servings

Porcupine Meatballs

START TO FINISH: 35 minutes

Prepping: 15 minutes
Cooking: 20 minutes

- 1 pound ground turkey
- 2 cups cooked brown **or** regular long-grain white rice
- 1 egg
- ¾ teaspoon dried oregano leaves, crushed
- ½ teaspoon garlic powder
- ¼ teaspoon ground black pepper
- 1 jar (1 pound 10 ounces) Prego® Traditional **or** Tomato, Basil & Garlic Pasta Sauce

1. Thoroughly mix the turkey, rice, egg, oregano, garlic powder and black pepper in a medium bowl.

2. Shape the mixture into 25 meatballs.

3. Heat the pasta sauce in a 12-inch skillet over medium-high heat. Add the meatballs in one layer. Heat to a boil. Reduce the heat to low. Cover and cook for 10 minutes or until meatballs are cooked through*.

Makes: 5 servings

*The internal temperature of the meatballs should reach 160°F.

Appetizers & Snacks

Single-Serve Southwest Dip Cups

START TO FINISH: 20 minutes

Prepping: 20 minutes

- 24 foil baking cups (2½-inch)
- 1 can (15.5 ounces) Pace® Refried Beans
- 2 jars (11 ounces **each**) Pace® Chunky Salsa
- 3 medium avocados, peeled and chopped (about 1½ cups)
- 1½ cups shredded Cheddar cheese (6 ounces)
- 1½ cups sour cream
- ½ cup chopped fresh cilantro leaves
- Bite-size tortilla chips

1. Place the foil cups on a serving platter.

2. Layer **about 1 tablespoon** each of the beans, salsa, avocado and cheese into **each** cup. Top each with a spoonful of sour cream and sprinkle with cilantro.

3. Serve with the chips for dipping.

Makes: 24 servings

Appetizers & Snacks

Soup's On

Creamy Citrus Tomato Soup with Pesto Croutons

START TO FINISH: 15 minutes

Prepping: 10 minutes
Cooking: 5 minutes

- 1 can (10¾ ounces) Campbell's® Condensed Tomato Soup
- 1 cup milk
- ½ cup light cream **or** half-and-half
- 1 tablespoon lemon juice
- 6 tablespoons prepared pesto
- 6 slices French **or** Italian bread, ½-inch thick, toasted

1. Stir the soup, milk, cream and lemon juice in a 2-quart saucepan. Heat the soup over medium heat until hot.

2. Spread **1 tablespoon** of the pesto on each toast slice.

3. Divide the soup among 6 serving bowls. Float a pesto crouton on each bowl of soup.

Makes: 6 servings

Roasted Tomato & Barley Soup

START TO FINISH: 1 hour 15 minutes

Prepping: 10 minutes
Baking: 25 minutes
Cooking: 40 minutes

- 1 can (28 ounces) diced tomatoes, undrained
- 2 large onions, diced (about 2 cups)
- 2 cloves garlic, minced
- 2 tablespoons olive oil
- 4 cups Swanson® Chicken Broth (Regular, Natural Goodness™ **or** Certified Organic)
- 2 stalks celery, diced (about 1 cup)
- ½ cup **uncooked** barley
- 2 tablespoons chopped fresh parsley

1. Heat the oven to 425°F. Drain the tomatoes, reserving the juice. Put the tomatoes, onions and garlic in a 17x11-inch roasting pan. Pour the oil over the vegetables and toss to coat. Bake for 25 minutes.

2. Put the roasted vegetables in a 3-quart saucepan. Add the reserved tomato juice, broth, celery and barley and heat to a boil. Cover and reduce the heat to low.

3. Cook for 35 minutes or until the barley is tender. Stir in the parsley.

Makes: 8 servings

Hearty Bean & Barley Soup

START TO FINISH: 55 minutes

Prepping: 15 minutes
Cooking: 40 minutes

- 1 tablespoon olive oil
- 2 large carrots, coarsely chopped
- 2 stalks celery, sliced
- 1 large onion, chopped
- 3 cloves garlic, minced
- 2 cans (14 ounces **each**) Swanson® Vegetable Broth
- 1 can (about 15 ounces) red kidney beans, drained and rinsed
- 1 can (14½ ounces) diced tomatoes
- ¼ cup **uncooked** pearl barley
- 2 cups firmly packed chopped fresh spinach leaves
- Ground black pepper

1. Heat the oil in a 4-quart saucepot over medium-high heat. Add the carrots, celery, onion and garlic. Cook and stir until the vegetables are tender.

2. Stir in the broth, beans, tomatoes and barley. Heat to a boil. Reduce the heat to low. Cover and cook for 30 minutes or until the barley is done.

3. Stir in the spinach and season to taste with black pepper. Heat through.

Makes: 6 servings

Soup's On

Chipotle Chili

START TO FINISH: 8 to 9 hours 15 minutes

Prepping: 15 minutes
Cooking: 8 to 9 hours

- 1 jar (16 ounces) Pace® Chipotle Chunky Salsa
- 1 cup water
- 2 tablespoons chili powder
- 1 large onion, chopped (about 1 cup)
- 2 pounds beef for stew, cut into ½-inch pieces
- 1 can (about 19 ounces) red kidney beans, rinsed and drained
- Shredded Cheddar cheese (optional)
- Sour cream (optional)

1. Stir the salsa, water, chili powder, onion, beef and beans in a 3½-quart slow cooker.

2. Cover and cook on LOW for 8 to 9 hours* or until the beef is fork-tender.

3. Serve with the cheese and sour cream, if desired.

Makes: 8 servings

*Or on HIGH for 4 to 5 hours

Soup's On

White Bean with Fennel Soup

START TO FINISH: 7 to 8 hours 15 minutes

Prepping: 15 minutes
Cooking: 7 to 8 hours

- 4 cups Swanson® Vegetable Broth (Regular **or** Certified Organic)
- 1/8 teaspoon ground black pepper
- 1 small bulb fennel (about 1/2 pound), trimmed and sliced (about 2 cups)
- 1 medium onion, chopped (about 1/2 cup)
- 2 cloves garlic, minced
- 1 package (10 ounces) frozen leaf spinach
- 1 can (14 1/2 ounces) diced tomatoes
- 1 can (about 16 ounces) white kidney (cannellini) beans, undrained

1. Stir the broth, black pepper, fennel, onion and garlic in a 5 1/2- to 6-quart slow cooker.

2. Cover and cook on LOW for 6 to 7 hours.

3. Add the spinach, tomatoes and undrained beans. Turn the heat to HIGH. Cover and cook for 1 hour more or until the vegetables are tender.

Makes: 6 servings

Spaghetti Soup

START TO FINISH: 45 minutes

Prepping: 15 minutes
Cooking: 30 minutes

- 2 tablespoons vegetable oil
- ½ pound skinless, boneless chicken breasts, cut into cubes
- 1 medium onion, chopped (about ½ cup)
- 1 large carrot, chopped (about ½ cup)
- 1 stalk celery, finely chopped (about ⅓ cup)
- 2 cloves garlic, minced
- 4 cups Swanson® Chicken Broth (Regular, Natural Goodness™ or Certified Organic)
- 1 can (10¾ ounces) Campbell's® Condensed Tomato Soup
- 1 cup water
- 3 ounces spaghetti, broken into 1-inch pieces
- 2 tablespoons chopped fresh parsley (optional)

1. Heat **1 tablespoon** oil in a saucepot over medium-high heat. Add the chicken and cook until it's browned, stirring often. Remove the chicken.

2. Stir in the remaining oil and heat over medium heat. Add the onion and cook for 1 minute. Add the carrots and cook for 1 minute. Add the celery and garlic and cook for 1 minute.

3. Stir in the broth, soup and water. Heat to a boil. Stir in the pasta. Cook for 10 minutes or until pasta is tender. Add the chicken and parsley, if desired, and heat through.

Makes: 4 servings

Soup's On

30-Minute Dishes

French Onion Burgers

START TO FINISH: 25 minutes

Prepping: 5 minutes
Cooking: 20 minutes

- 1 pound ground beef
- 1 can (10½ ounces) Campbell's® Condensed French Onion Soup
- 4 slices cheese
- 4 round hard rolls, split

1. Shape the beef into 4 (½-inch) thick burgers.

2. Heat a 10-inch skillet over medium-high heat. Add the burgers and cook until they're well browned on both sides. Remove the burgers and set aside. Pour off any fat.

3. Stir in the soup into the skillet. Heat to a boil. Return the burgers to the skillet and reduce the heat to low. Cover and cook for 5 minutes or until the burgers are cooked through*. Top with cheese and continue cooking until the cheese melts. Serve burgers in rolls with soup mixture for dipping.

Makes: 4 burgers

*The internal temperature of the burgers should reach 160°F.

Grilled Pork in Pitas

START TO FINISH: 25 minutes

Prepping: 10 minutes
Grilling: 15 minutes

- ¾ cup Pace® Picante Sauce
- ½ cup plain yogurt
- 1 teaspoon lime juice
- ¼ teaspoon garlic powder **or** 2 cloves garlic, minced
- 1 pound boneless pork chops, ¾-inch thick
- 6 pita breads (6-inch), warmed
- 1 cup shredded lettuce
- 1 medium green onion, sliced (about 2 tablespoons)

1. Mix **3 tablespoons** picante sauce, yogurt and lime juice. Refrigerate until ready to serve. Mix the remaining picante sauce and garlic powder in a small bowl.

2. Lightly oil the grill rack and heat the grill to medium-high. Grill the pork chops for 15 minutes or until chops are cooked through but slightly pink in center*, turning and brushing them often with the picante sauce mixture while they're grilling. Discard remaining picante sauce mixture.

3. Slice the pork into thin strips. Spoon the pork down the center of the pita. Top with the yogurt mixture, lettuce and green onion. Fold pita around filling.

Makes: 6 sandwiches

*The internal temperature of the pork should reach 160°F.

Time-Saving Tip: To warm the pita breads, wrap them in a plain paper towel. Microwave on HIGH for 1 minute or until warm.

Southwest Salsa Chicken with Fresh Greens

START TO FINISH: 20 minutes

Prepping: 10 minutes
Cooking: 10 minutes

1	tablespoon chili powder
1	teaspoon ground cumin
1½	pounds skinless, boneless chicken breast halves, cut into strips
1	tablespoon olive oil
1	cup Pace® Chunky Salsa
¼	cup water
1	bag (about 7 ounces) mixed salad greens (6 cups)

1. Mix the chili powder and cumin in a shallow dish. Coat the chicken with the seasonings.

2. Heat the oil in a heavy 12-inch skillet over high heat. Add the chicken and cook until the chicken is blackened and cooked through*, stirring often. Remove the chicken and set aside.

3. Stir in the salsa and water. Cook and stir over medium heat until mixture is hot and bubbling. Divide the salad greens among 6 plates. Top each with chicken and salsa.

Makes: 6 servings

*The internal temperature of the chicken should reach 160°F.

Beef 'n' Bean Burritos

START TO FINISH: 15 minutes

Prepping: 5 minutes
Cooking/Baking: 10 minutes

- 1 pound ground beef
- 1 small onion, chopped (about ¼ cup)
- 1 can (11.25 ounces) Campbell's® Condensed Fiesta Chili Beef Soup
- ¼ cup water
- 8 flour tortillas (8-inch), warmed
  Shredded Cheddar cheese
  Pace® Chunky Salsa
  Sour cream

1. Cook the beef and onion in a 10-inch skillet over medium-high heat until the beef is well browned, stirring frequently to break up meat. Pour off any fat.

2. Stir in the soup and water. Cook until the mixture is hot and bubbling.

3. Spoon **about ⅓ cup** of the beef mixture down the center of each tortilla. Top with cheese, salsa and sour cream. Fold the sides of the tortilla over the filling and then fold up the ends to enclose the filling.

Makes: 8 burritos

30-Minute Dishes

Italian Fish Fillets

START TO FINISH: 20 minutes

Prepping: 10 minutes
Baking: 10 minutes

- 2 slices Pepperidge Farm® Sandwich White Bread, torn into pieces
- 1/3 cup shredded Parmesan cheese
- 1 clove garlic
- 1/2 teaspoon dried thyme leaves, crushed
- 1/8 teaspoon ground black pepper
- 2 tablespoons olive oil
- 8 fresh tilapia fish fillets (3 to 4 ounces **each**)
- 1 egg, beaten

1. Place the bread, cheese, garlic, thyme and black pepper in an electric blender container. Cover and blend until fine crumbs form. Slowly add the olive oil and blend until moistened.

2. Put the fish fillets in a 17×11-inch roasting pan. Brush with the egg. Divide the bread crumb mixture evenly over the fillets.

3. Bake at 400°F. for 10 minutes or until the fish flakes easily when tested with a fork and the crumb topping is golden.

Makes: 8 servings

Easy Substitution Tip: Substitute about 2 pounds firm white fish fillets such as cod, haddock or halibut for the tilapia fillets.

Quick Ranchero Chili

START TO FINISH: 25 minutes

Prepping: 5 minutes
Cooking: 20 minutes

1	pound ground beef
1	medium onion, chopped (about ½ cup)
2	tablespoons chili powder
1	can (10¾ ounces) Campbell's® Condensed Creamy Ranchero Tomato Soup
½	cup water
1	can (about 15 ounces) small red beans **or** red kidney beans, rinsed and drained
	Shredded Cheddar cheese

1. Cook the beef, onion and chili powder in a 10-inch skillet over medium-high heat until the beef is well browned, stirring frequently to break up the meat. Pour off any fat.

2. Stir in the soup, water and beans and heat to a boil.

3. Cover and reduce the heat to low. Cook for 10 minutes. Top with the cheese.

Makes: 4 servings

30-Minute Dishes

Quick Chicken Parmesan

START TO FINISH: 15 minutes

Prepping: 5 minutes
Baking: 10 minutes

- 2 cups Prego® Traditional Pasta Sauce
- 4 fully cooked breaded chicken cutlets
- 4 thin slices cooked ham
- 1 cup shredded mozzarella cheese (4 ounces)
- 2 tablespoons grated Parmesan cheese

1. Spread **1 cup** of the pasta sauce in a 12×8×2-inch shallow baking dish.

2. Place the chicken cutlets over the sauce. Spoon ¼ **cup** of the remaining pasta sauce down the center of each cutlet. Top each with **1 slice** ham and ¼ **cup** mozzarella cheese. Sprinkle with the Parmesan cheese.

3. Bake at 425°F. for 10 minutes or until the cheese melts and the sauce is hot and bubbly.

Makes: 4 servings

30-Minute Dishes

Tomato-Basil Chicken

START TO FINISH: 25 minutes

Prepping: 10 minutes
Cooking: 15 minutes

- 1 tablespoon vegetable oil
- 1½ pounds skinless, boneless chicken breast halves (about 4 to 6)
- 1 can (10¾ ounces) Campbell's® Condensed Tomato Soup
- ½ cup milk
- 2 tablespoons grated Parmesan cheese
- ½ teaspoon dried basil leaves, crushed
- ¼ teaspoon garlic powder **or** 2 cloves garlic, minced
- 3 cups medium tube-shaped pasta (ziti), cooked and drained

1. Heat the oil in a 10-inch skillet over medium-high heat. Add the chicken and cook for 10 minutes or until it's well browned on both sides. Remove the chicken and set aside.

2. Stir in the soup, milk, cheese, basil and garlic powder. Heat to a boil. Return the chicken to the skillet and reduce the heat to low. Cover and cook for 5 minutes or until the chicken is cooked through*.

3. Serve with the pasta.

Makes: 6 servings

*The internal temperature of the chicken should reach 160°F.

Family Favorites

Potato Crusted Chicken

START TO FINISH: 35 minutes

Prepping: 10 minutes
Baking: 25 minutes

    Vegetable cooking spray
1   package (about 4 ounces) butter-flavored instant mashed potatoes flakes (about 1¼ cups)
½   cup shredded Cheddar cheese
2   teaspoons dried oregano leaves, crushed
⅓   cup mayonnaise
3   pounds skinless, boneless chicken breast halves (about 8 to 10)

1. Heat the oven to 400°F. Spray a baking sheet with the cooking spray.

2. Mix the potatoes, cheese and oregano in a shallow bowl. Brush the mayonnaise on both sides of the chicken. Dip the chicken into the potato mixture to coat well on both sides. Place the chicken on the prepared pan.

3. Bake for 25 minutes or until chicken is cooked through* and coating is golden brown.

Makes: 12 servings

*The internal temperature of the chicken should reach 160°F.

Beef Stroganoff

START TO FINISH: 20 minutes

Prepping: 10 minutes
Cooking: 10 minutes

- 1 pound boneless beef sirloin **or** top round steak, ¾-inch thick, cut into 2-inch pieces
- Cracked black pepper
- 1 tablespoon vegetable oil
- 1 medium onion, finely chopped (about ½ cup)
- 1 can (10¾ ounces) Campbell's® Condensed Cream of Mushroom Soup (Regular **or** 98% Fat Free)
- ½ cup water
- ¼ cup dry sherry (optional)
- 1 tablespoon tomato paste
- ¼ cup plain yogurt
- Hot cooked medium egg noodles
- Chopped fresh parsley

1. Sprinkle the beef with the black pepper.

2. Heat the oil in a 10-inch skillet over medium-high heat. Add the beef and cook until it's well browned on all sides, stirring often. Remove the beef with a slotted spoon and set it aside.

3. Reduce the heat to medium. Add the onion. Cook and stir until the onion is tender. Stir in the soup, water, sherry, if desired, and tomato paste. Heat to a boil. Return the beef to the skillet and heat through. Remove from the heat. Stir in the yogurt. Serve over the noodles and sprinkle with the parsley.

Makes: 4 servings

Ranchero Oven-Fried Chicken

START TO FINISH: 1 hour

Prepping: 10 minutes
Baking: 50 minutes

- 2 cups Pepperidge Farm® Herb Seasoned **or** Corn Bread Stuffing, crushed
- ½ cup all-purpose flour
- 1 can (10¾ ounces) Campbell's® Condensed Creamy Ranchero Tomato Soup
- 1 tablespoon water
- 4 pounds chicken parts (breasts, thighs, drumsticks)

1. Put the crushed stuffing and flour on 2 separate plates.

2. Stir the soup and water in a shallow dish. Lightly coat the chicken with the flour. Dip the chicken into the soup mixture, then coat with the stuffing crumbs.

3. Put the chicken on a baking sheet. Bake at 400°F. for 50 minutes or until the chicken is cooked through*. Serve the chicken warm or at room temperature.

Makes: 8 servings

*The internal temperature of the chicken parts should reach 170°F.

Cooking for a Crowd: Recipe may be doubled.

Make Ahead: Prepare the chicken as directed and cool for 30 minutes. Cover and refrigerate the chicken for up to 24 hours. When ready to serve, place the chicken on a baking sheet and bake at 350°F. for 30 minutes or until hot.

Family Favorites

Cranberry Dijon Pork Chops

START TO FINISH: 55 minutes

Prepping: 10 minutes
Cooking/Baking: 45 minutes

- 1 tablespoon olive oil
- 4 boneless pork chops, 1-inch thick (about 1¼ pounds)
- 1 can (10¾ ounces) Campbell's® Condensed Cream of Celery Soup (Regular **or** 98% Fat Free)
- ½ cup cranberry juice
- 2 tablespoons Dijon-style mustard
- ¼ teaspoon dried thyme leaves, crushed
- ¼ cup dried cranberries **or** cherries
- Hot cooked noodles

1. Heat the oil in a 10-inch oven-safe skillet over medium-high heat. Add the pork chops and cook until the chops are well browned on both sides. Remove the pork chops and set them aside.

2. Stir in the soup, cranberry juice, mustard and thyme. Heat to a boil. Return the pork chops to the skillet and cover.

3. Bake at 350°F. for 45 minutes or until chops are cooked through but slightly pink in center*. Place the pork chops on a serving plate. Stir the cranberries into the skillet. Serve the sauce with the pork and noodles.

Makes: 4 servings

*The internal temperature of the pork should reach 160°F.

Chicken Nacho Tacos

START TO FINISH: 25 minutes

Prepping: 10 minutes
Cooking: 15 minutes

- 1 tablespoon vegetable oil
- 1 medium onion, chopped (about ½ cup)
- ½ teaspoon chili powder
- 1 can (11 ounces) Campbell's® Condensed Fiesta Nacho Cheese Soup
- 2 cans (4.5 ounces **each**) Swanson® Premium Chunk Chicken Breast, drained
- 8 taco shells **or** flour tortillas (6 inch), warmed
- Shredded lettuce **and** chopped tomato

1. Heat the oil in a 10-inch skillet over medium heat. Add the onion and chili powder and cook until the onion is tender.

2. Stir in the soup and chicken. Cook and stir until it's hot.

3. Divide the chicken mixture among the taco shells. Top with the lettuce and tomato.

Makes: 8 tacos

Holiday Fun

Green Bean Casserole

START TO FINISH: 40 minutes

Prepping: 10 minutes
Baking: 30 minutes

- 1 can (10¾ ounces) Campbell's® Condensed Cream of Mushroom Soup (Regular **or** 98% Fat Free)
- ½ cup milk
- 1 teaspoon soy sauce
- Dash ground black pepper
- 2 packages (10 ounces **each**) frozen cut green beans, cooked and drained
- 1 can (2.8 ounces) French fried onions (1⅓ cups)

1. Stir the soup, milk, soy, black pepper, green beans and ⅔ **cup** onions in a 1½-quart casserole.

2. Bake at 350°F. for 25 minutes or until hot. Stir the green bean mixture.

3. Sprinkle the remaining onions over the green bean mixture. Bake for 5 minutes more or until onions are golden brown.

Makes: 5 servings

Holiday Potato Pancakes

START TO FINISH: 55 minutes

Prepping: 25 minutes
Cooking: 30 minutes

- 8 medium potatoes, (about 3 pounds), peeled and grated (about 7 cups)
- 2 cans (10¾ ounces **each**) Campbell's® Condensed Broccoli Cheese Soup
- 3 eggs, beaten
- 2 tablespoons all-purpose flour
- ¼ teaspoon freshly ground black pepper
- ½ cup vegetable oil
- Sour cream
- Chopped chives

1. Wrap the grated potatoes in a clean dish or paper towel. Twist the towel and squeeze to wring out as much of the liquid as possible.

2. Mix the soup, eggs, flour, black pepper and potatoes in a 3-quart bowl.

3. Heat ¼ **cup** oil in a deep nonstick 12-inch skillet over medium-high heat. Drop a scant ¼ **cup** potato mixture into the pan, making **4** pancakes at a time. Press on each pancake to flatten to 3 or 4 inches. Cook for 4 minutes, turning once or until the pancakes are dark golden brown. Remove the pancakes and keep warm. Repeat with the remaining potato mixture, adding more of the remaining oil as needed. Serve with the sour cream and chives.

Makes: 36 pancakes

Herb Roasted Turkey

START TO FINISH: 4 to 4½ hours 55 minutes

Prepping: 15 minutes
Roasting: 4 to 4½ hours 30 minutes
Standing: 10 minutes

- 1¾ cups Swanson® Chicken Broth (Regular, Natural Goodness™ **or** Certified Organic)
- 3 tablespoons lemon juice
- 1 teaspoon dried basil leaves, crushed
- 1 teaspoon dried thyme leaves, crushed
- ⅛ teaspoon ground black pepper
- 12- to 14-pound turkey
- 2 cans (14½ ounces **each**) Campbell's™ Turkey Gravy

1. Mix the broth, lemon juice, basil, thyme and black pepper in a medium bowl.

2. Roast the turkey according to package directions*, basting occasionally with the broth mixture. Let the turkey stand for 10 minutes before slicing. Discard any remaining broth mixture.

3. Heat the gravy and serve with the turkey.

Makes: 12 to 14 servings

*The internal temperature of the turkey should reach 180°F.

Heavenly Sweet Potatoes

START TO FINISH: 30 minutes

Prepping: 10 minutes
Baking: 20 minutes

Vegetable cooking spray
1 can (40 ounces) cut sweet potatoes in heavy syrup, drained
¼ teaspoon ground cinnamon
⅛ teaspoon ground ginger
¾ cup Swanson® Chicken Broth (Regular, Natural Goodness™ or Certified Organic)
2 cups miniature marshmallows

1. Spray a 1½-quart casserole with cooking spray. Set the dish aside.

2. Place the potatoes, cinnamon and ginger in a 3-quart bowl. Beat with an electric mixer on medium speed until the potatoes are fluffy and almost smooth. Add the broth and beat until the ingredients are mixed. Spoon the potato mixture into the prepared dish. Top with the marshmallows.

3. Bake at 350°F. for 20 minutes or until hot and marshmallows are golden brown.

Makes: 8 servings

Layered Cranberry Walnut Stuffing

START TO FINISH: 35 minutes

Prepping: 10 minutes
Baking: 25 minutes

- 2 boxes (6 ounces **each**) Pepperidge Farm® Stuffing Mix
- 1½ cups Swanson® Chicken Broth (Regular, Natural Goodness™ or Certified Organic)
- 2 tablespoons butter
- 1 can (16 ounces) whole cranberry sauce
- ½ cup walnuts, toasted and chopped

1. Prepare the stuffing using the broth and butter according to the package directions.

2. Spoon **half** of the stuffing into a 2-quart casserole. Spoon **half** of the cranberry sauce over the stuffing. Sprinkle with ¼ **cup** walnuts. Repeat the layers.

3. Bake at 350°F. for 25 minutes or until hot.

Makes: 6 servings

Holiday Fun

Swiss Vegetable Bake

START TO FINISH: 50 minutes

Prepping: 5 minutes
Baking: 45 minutes

- 1 can (26 ounces) Campbell's® Condensed Cream of Chicken Soup
- ⅔ cup sour cream
- ½ teaspoon ground black pepper
- 2 bags (16 ounces **each**) frozen vegetable combination (broccoli, cauliflower, carrots), thawed
- 2 cups shredded Swiss cheese (8 ounces)
- 1 can (6 ounces) French fried onions (2⅔ cups)

1. Stir the soup, sour cream, black pepper, vegetables, **1½ cups** cheese and **1⅓ cups** onions in a 13×9×2-inch shallow baking dish and cover.

2. Bake at 350°F. for 40 minutes or until the vegetables are tender. Stir the vegetable mixture.

3. Sprinkle the remaining cheese and onions over the vegetable mixture. Bake for 5 minutes more or until the onions are golden brown.

Makes: 8 servings

Time-Saving Tip: To thaw the vegetables, cut off 1 corner on bag, microwave on HIGH for 5 minutes.

Goblin's Toes

START TO FINISH: 1 hour 10 minutes

Thawing: 40 minutes
Prepping: 10 minutes
Baking: 20 minutes

- ½ of a 17.3 ounce package Pepperidge Farm® Frozen Puff Pastry Sheets (1 sheet)
- 1 package (14 ounces) cocktail franks (about 30)
- ¼ cup prepared mustard
- ¼ cup ketchup

1. Thaw the pastry sheet at room temperature for 40 minutes or until it's easy to handle. Heat the oven to 375°F. Lightly grease a baking sheet.

2. Unfold the pastry sheet on a lightly floured surface. Cut it in half lengthwise. Cut each half crosswise into 15 (½-inch-wide) strips. Wrap one end of each cocktail frank with one pastry strip, overlapping slightly to resemble a "bandage." Put them on a baking sheet about 1 inch apart.

3. Bake for 20 minutes or until the pastry is golden. Remove the cocktail franks from the baking sheet and cool them slightly on a wire rack. Dollop some mustard on toes. Serve with remaining mustard and ketchup for dipping.

Makes: 30 appetizers

Bloody Fingers

START TO FINISH: 20 minutes

Prepping: 15 minutes
Baking: 5 minutes

- 24 sliced blanched almonds
- Red liquid **or** paste food coloring
- 2 packages (about 9 ounces **each**) refrigerated fully cooked breaded chicken strips (about 24)
- 1 egg, slightly beaten
- 1 jar (1 pound 10 ounces) Prego® Traditional Pasta Sauce

1. Heat the oven to 400°F. Brush the almonds with the food coloring to coat. Set them aside to dry, about 10 minutes.

2. Place the chicken strips on a baking sheet. Brush the narrow end of the chicken strips with egg and press almonds on the egg wash to attach. Bake for 5 minutes or until hot.

3. Pour the pasta sauce in a 2-quart saucepan over medium heat. Cook until it's hot and bubbling, stirring occasionally. Arrange the chicken on a serving platter. Serve with the sauce for dipping.

Makes: 8 servings

Easy Substitution Tip: Substitute frozen fully cooked breaded chicken strips for the refrigerated chicken strips. Increase the bake time to 10 minutes.

Holiday Fun

Vegetables and Sides

Cheddar Broccoli Bake

START TO FINISH: 40 minutes

Prepping: 10 minutes
Baking: 30 minutes

- 1 can (10¾ ounces) Campbell's® Condensed Cheddar Cheese Soup
- ½ cup milk
- Dash ground black pepper
- 4 cups cooked broccoli cuts
- 1 can (2.8 ounces) French fried onions (1⅓ cups)

1. Stir the soup, milk, black pepper, broccoli and ⅔ **cup** onions in a 1½-quart casserole and cover.

2. Bake at 350°F. for 25 minutes or until hot. Stir the broccoli mixture.

3. Sprinkle the remaining onions over the broccoli mixture. Bake for 5 minutes more or until the onions are golden.

Makes: 6 servings

Glazed Snow Peas and Carrots

START TO FINISH: 25 minutes

Prepping: 10 minutes
Cooking: 15 minutes

- 4 teaspoons cornstarch
- 1¾ cups Swanson® Vegetable Broth (Regular **or** Certified Organic)
- 4 medium carrots, sliced (about 2 cups)
- 1 medium onion, chopped (about ½ cup)
- ¾ pound snow peas
- 1 teaspoon lemon juice

1. Stir the cornstarch and **1 cup** broth in a small cup. Set the mixture aside.

2. Heat the remaining broth in a 10-inch skillet over medium-high heat to a boil. Add the carrots and onion and reduce the heat to low. Cover and cook for 5 minutes or until the carrots are tender-crisp. Add the snow peas and cook for 2 minutes.

3. Stir the cornstarch mixture and stir it into the skillet. Cook and stir until the mixture boils and thickens. Stir in the lemon juice.

Makes: 8 servings

Mediterranean Chop Salad

START TO FINISH: 25 minutes

Prepping: 25 minutes

- 1 package (12 ounces) romaine lettuce hearts, chopped
- 1 large seedless cucumber, peeled and chopped (about 1⅔ cups)
- 3 stalks celery, sliced **or** 1 cup sliced fennel (about 1½ cups)
- 1 cup chopped roasted red **or** yellow sweet peppers
- ½ cup chopped pitted ripe olives
- 1 box (6 ounces) Pepperidge Farm® Croutons, any variety
- ½ cup prepared balsamic vinaigrette dressing
- Freshly ground black pepper
- Parmesan cheese shavings

1. Mix the lettuce, cucumber, celery, red pepper, olives and croutons in a 4-quart serving bowl.

2. Pour the dressing over the vegetables, tossing until well coated.

3. Serve immediately with the black pepper and cheese.

Makes: 8 to 10 servings

Vegetables and Sides

Toasted Corn & Sage Harvest Risotto

START TO FINISH: 50 minutes

Prepping: 15 minutes
Cooking: 35 minutes

- 1 tablespoon olive oil
- 1 cup fresh **or** drained, canned whole kernel corn
- 1 large orange **or** red pepper, chopped (about 1 cup)
- 1 medium onion, chopped (about ½ cup)
- 1¾ cups **uncooked** regular long-grain white rice
- 4 cups Swanson® Chicken, Natural Goodness™ Chicken **or** Vegetable Broth
- 1 teaspoon ground sage
- 1 can (10¾ ounces) Campbell's® Condensed Cream of Celery Soup (Regular **or** 98% Fat Free)
- ¼ cup grated Parmesan cheese

1. Heat the oil in a 4-quart saucepan over medium heat. Add the corn, pepper and onion and cook for 6 minutes or until the vegetables start to brown.

2. Add the rice and cook for 30 seconds, stirring constantly. Stir in the broth and sage and heat to a boil. Reduce the heat to low. Cover the saucepan and cook for 20 minutes or until the rice is done and most of the liquid is absorbed.

3. Stir in the soup. Cook for 2 minutes more, stirring occasionally until heated through. Sprinkle with cheese.

Makes: 16 servings

Spaghetti Squash Alfredo

START TO FINISH: 1 hour 10 minutes

Prepping: 10 minutes
Baking/Cooking: 1 hour

- 1 medium spaghetti squash (about 3 pounds)
- 1 can (10¾ ounces) Campbell's® Condensed Cream of Celery Soup (Regular **or** 98% Fat Free)
- ¾ cup water
- ¼ cup milk
- 1 cup shredded low-fat Swiss cheese (4 ounces)
- 2 tablespoons grated Parmesan cheese
- Chopped fresh parsley **or** chives

1. Pierce squash with fork or skewer in several places. Bake at 350°F. for 50 minutes or until the squash is fork-tender. Cut in half, scoop out and discard seeds. Scrape the flesh with fork to separate the spaghetti-like strands.

2. Stir the soup, water and milk in a 2-quart saucepan. Heat over medium heat to a boil. Stir in the Swiss cheese.

3. Place the hot spaghetti squash in a 2-quart serving bowl. Pour the soup mixture over the squash. Toss to coat. Sprinkle with Parmesan cheese and parsley.

Makes: 5 servings

Broccoli & Noodles Supreme

START TO FINISH: 30 minutes

Prepping: 10 minutes
Cooking: 20 minutes

- 3 cups **uncooked** medium egg noodles
- 2 cups broccoli flowerets
- 1 can (10¾ ounces) Campbell's® Condensed Cream of Chicken Soup (Regular **or** 98% Fat Free)
- ½ cup sour cream
- ⅓ cup grated Parmesan cheese
- ⅛ teaspoon ground black pepper

1. Prepare the noodles according to the package directions in a 4-quart saucepot. Add the broccoli during the last 5 minutes of the cooking time. Drain the noodles and broccoli well in a colander and return them to the saucepot.

2. Stir the soup, sour cream, cheese and black pepper into the noodles and broccoli. Cook and stir over medium heat until hot.

3. Top with additional cheese before serving.

Makes: 5 servings

Mozzarella Zucchini Skillet

START TO FINISH: 25 minutes

Prepping: 10 minutes
Cooking: 15 minutes

- 2 tablespoons vegetable oil
- 5 medium zucchini, sliced (about 7½ cups)
- 1 medium onion, chopped (about ½ cup)
- ¼ teaspoon garlic powder **or** 2 cloves garlic, minced
- 1½ cups Prego® Traditional Pasta Sauce
- ½ cup shredded mozzarella **or** Cheddar cheese

1. Heat the oil in a 12-inch skillet over medium-high heat. Add the zucchini, onion and garlic powder and cook until the vegetables are tender-crisp.

2. Stir in the pasta sauce and heat through.

3. Sprinkle with the cheese. Cover and cook until the cheese melts.

Makes: 7 servings

Vegetables and Sides

Crab and Asparagus Risotto

START TO FINISH: 35 minutes

Prepping/Cooking: 30 minutes
Standing: 5 minutes

- 2 tablespoons olive oil
- 1 medium orange pepper, diced (about 1 cup)
- ½ cup chopped onion **or** shallots
- 2 cups **uncooked** Arborio rice (short-grain)
- ½ cup dry white wine
- 6 cups Swanson® Chicken Broth (Regular, Natural Goodness™ **or** Certified Organic), heated
- ½ pound asparagus **or** green beans, trimmed, cut into 1-inch pieces (about 1½ cups)
- ½ pound refrigerated pasteurized crabmeat (about 1½ cups)
- ¼ cup grated Parmesan cheese

1. Heat the oil in a 4-quart saucepan over medium heat. Add the pepper and onion and cook for 3 minutes or until the vegetables are tender. Add the rice and cook and stir for 2 minutes or until the rice is opaque.

2. Add the wine and cook and stir until it's absorbed. Stir **2 cups** of the hot broth into the rice mixture. Cook and stir until the broth is absorbed, maintaining the rice at a gentle simmer. Continue cooking and adding broth, ½ cup at a time, stirring until it's absorbed after each addition before adding more. Add the asparagus and crabmeat with the last broth addition.

3. Stir the cheese into the risotto. Remove the saucepan from the heat. Cover and let it stand for 5 minutes. Serve the risotto with additional cheese.

Makes: 8 servings

Sweet Treats

Fishy Families

START TO FINISH: 36 minutes 15 seconds

Prepping: 5 minutes
Cooking: 1 minute 15 seconds
Refrigerating: 30 minutes

- 1 package (12 ounces) semi-sweet chocolate pieces (2 cups)
- 2½ cups Pepperidge Farm® Pretzel Goldfish® Baked Snack Crackers
- 1 container (4 ounces) multi-colored nonpareils

1. Line a baking sheet with waxed paper and set it aside. Place the chocolate in a microwavable bowl. Microwave on HIGH for 1 minute. Stir. Microwave at 15 second intervals, stirring after each, until the chocolate melts. Stir in the crackers to coat.

2. Scoop up the cracker mixture with a tablespoon and drop onto the prepared baking sheet. Sprinkle with the nonpareils. Repeat with the remaining cracker mixture and nonpareils.

3. Refrigerate for 30 minutes or until the mixture is firm. Store in the refrigerator.

Makes: 1 pound

Chocolate and Coconut Cream Fondue

START TO FINISH: 15 minutes

Prepping: 5 minutes
Cooking: 10 minutes

- 1 can (15 ounces) cream of coconut
- 2 tablespoons rum (optional) **or** 1 teaspoon rum extract
- 1 package (12 ounces) semi-sweet chocolate pieces

Suggested Dippers: Assorted Pepperidge Farm® Cookies, Pepperidge Farm® Giant Goldfish® Grahams, whole strawberries, banana chunks, dried pineapple pieces **and/or** fresh pineapple chunks

1. Stir the cream of coconut, rum and chocolate in a 2-quart saucepan. Heat over medium heat until the chocolate melts, stirring occasionally.

2. Pour the chocolate mixture into a fondue pot or slow cooker.

3. Serve warm with the *Suggested Dippers*.

Makes: 3 cups

Leftover Tip: Any remaining fondue can be used as an ice cream or dessert topping. Cover and refrigerate in an airtight container. Reheat in saucepot until warm.

I'm Dreamy for White Chocolate Fondue

START TO FINISH: 15 minutes

Prepping: 5 minutes
Cooking: 10 minutes

- ⅓ cup heavy cream
- 1 tablespoon orange-flavored liqueur **or** ½ teaspoon orange extract
- 1 package (about 12 ounces) white chocolate pieces

Suggested Dippers: Assorted Pepperidge Farm® Cookies, whole strawberries, banana chunks, dried pineapple pieces **and/or** fresh pineapple chunks

1. Stir the cream, liqueur and chocolate in a 1-quart saucepan. Heat over low heat until the chocolate melts, stirring occasionally.

2. Pour the chocolate mixture into a fondue pot or slow cooker.

3. Serve warm with the *Suggested Dippers*.

Makes: 1½ cups

Bourbon Orange Chocolate Lady Dessert

START TO FINISH: 1 hour

Prepping: 15 minutes
Freezing: 45 minutes

- 2 fluid ounces (4 tablespoons) bourbon **or** orange juice
- 1 bag (7 ounces) Pepperidge Farm® Orange Milano® Distinctive Cookies, crushed
- 1 pint chocolate ice cream, softened
- Orange slices
- Orange peel

1. Heat the bourbon in a 1-quart saucepan over high heat to a boil. Reduce the heat to low. Cook for 3 minutes. Remove from heat and let cool. Crush **3** of the cookies.

2. Mix the bourbon, ice cream and crushed cookies in a 1-quart bowl.

3. Freeze for 45 minutes or until the mixture is firm. Scoop into dessert dishes. Garnish with orange slices, orange peel and remaining whole cookies, if desired.

Makes: 4 servings

Cooking for a Crowd: Recipe may be doubled.

Sweet Treats

Chocolate Cherry Ice Cream Cake

START TO FINISH: 2 hours 25 minutes

Prepping: 10 minutes
Freezing: 2 hours 15 minutes

- 1 package (6 ounces) Pepperidge Farm® Milano® Distinctive Cookies
- 1 container (1.75 quarts) black cherry ice cream
- 2 jars (17 ounces **each**) chocolate ice cream sauce
- 1 container (1.75 quarts) vanilla ice cream
- Sweetened whipped cream for garnish
- Frozen pitted dark cherries, thawed for garnish

1. Stand **10** of the cookies on their sides along the edge of a 9-inch springform pan, forming a ring. Coarsely chop the remaining cookies.

2. Spoon the black cherry ice cream into the pan and spread into an even layer. Spoon **1** jar of the chocolate sauce over the ice cream. Sprinkle with the coarsely chopped cookies. Freeze for 15 minutes.

3. Evenly spread the vanilla ice cream over the cookie layer. Pour the remaining chocolate sauce in the center, spreading into a circle to within 1 inch of the edge. Pipe the whipped cream around the top edge. Freeze for 2 hours more or until the mixture is firm. Place the cherries on top of the chocolate sauce just before serving.

Makes: 10 servings

Sweet Treats

Mini Chocolate Cookie Cheesecakes

START TO FINISH: 3 hours 40 minutes

Prepping: 20 minutes
Baking: 20 minutes
Cooling: 1 hour
Refrigerating: 2 hours

- 16 foil baking cups (2½-inch)
- 2 packages (4.9 ounces **each**) Pepperidge Farm® Mini Milano® Distinctive Cookies
- 2 packages (8 ounces **each**) cream cheese, softened
- ½ cup sugar
- 2 eggs
- ½ teaspoon vanilla extract

1. Heat the oven to 350°F. Put the foil baking cups into 16 (2½-inch) muffin-pan cups or on a baking sheet. Place **2** cookies in the bottom of each cup and set aside. Cut the remaining cookies in half.

2. Beat the cream cheese, sugar, eggs and vanilla in a medium bowl with an electric mixer on medium speed until smooth. Spoon the cheese mixture into the baking cups filling each cup ¾ full. Insert **2** cookie halves, with the cut ends down, into the cheese mixture of each cup.

3. Bake for 20 minutes or until the centers are set. Cool the cheesecakes on a wire rack for 1 hour. Refrigerate the cheesecakes for at least 2 hours before serving.

Makes: 16 servings

Southern Pecan Crisps

START TO FINISH: 1 hour 47 minutes

Thawing: 40 minutes
Prepping: 25 minutes
Baking: 12 minutes
Cooling: 30 minutes

- ½ of a 17.3 ounce package Pepperidge Farm® Frozen Puff Pastry Sheets (1 sheet)
- ½ cup packed brown sugar
- ⅓ cup pecan halves, chopped
- 2 tablespoons butter, melted
- Confectioners' sugar

1. Thaw the pastry sheet at room temperature for 40 minutes or until it's easy to handle. Heat the oven to 400°F. Mix the brown sugar and the pecans with the butter in a small bowl.

2. Unfold the pastry sheet on a lightly floured surface. Roll the sheet into a 15×12-inch rectangle. Cut the pastry into (20) 3-inch squares. Press the squares into bottoms of 3-inch muffin-pan cups. Place **1 heaping teaspoon** pecan mixture in the center of **each** cup.

3. Bake for 12 minutes or until golden. Remove the pastry from the pans and cool on a wire rack. Sprinkle the pastries with the confectioners' sugar before serving.

Makes: 20 pastries

Quick & Easy Berry Shortcakes

START TO FINISH: 2 hours 20 minutes

Prepping: 10 minutes
Baking: 40 minutes
Cooling: 1 hour 30 minutes

- 1 box (16 ounces) angel food cake mix
- 1¾ cups Diet V8 Splash® Berry Blend Juice
- 6 cups cut-up fresh strawberries, blueberries **and** raspberries
- 1½ cups thawed light whipped topping

1. Heat the oven to 350°F. Prepare the cake mix according to the package directions, substituting juice for the water. Pour the batter into a 10-inch tube pan.

2. Bake for 40 minutes or until the top is golden brown and springs back when lightly touched with a finger. The cracks in the top of the cake should look dry. Invert the cake in the pan and hang upside down on a funnel or heatproof glass bottle for about 1½ hours to cool completely.

3. Loosen cake from pan with a metal spatula. Cut the cake into **24** slices. For each serving, place **1** cake slice on a serving plate, top with ¼ **cup** berries and **1 tablespoon** whipped topping, top with another cake slice, ¼ **cup** berries and **1 tablespoon** whipped topping. Repeat with remaining cake slices, berries and whipped topping.

Makes: 12 servings

Sweet Treats

Super Chunky Fudge

START TO FINISH: 2 hours 25 minutes

Prepping: 15 minutes
Cooking: 10 minutes
Refrigerating: 2 hours

- 1 bag (5.1 ounces) Pepperidge Farm® Mini Chocolate Chunk Cookies, coarsely crumbled (about 2 cups)
- 1 cup miniature marshmallows
- Vegetable cooking spray
- 3 cups semi-sweet chocolate pieces (18 ounces)
- 1 can (14 ounces) sweetened condensed milk
- 1/8 teaspoon salt
- 1 teaspoon vanilla extract

1. Reserve ½ **cup** crumbled cookies and ¼ **cup** marshmallows. Line an 8-inch square baking pan with foil. Spray the foil with cooking spray. Heat the chocolate, milk and salt in a 2-quart saucepan over low heat until the chocolate melts, stirring often.

2. Remove the chocolate mixture from the heat and stir in remaining crumbled cookies, remaining marshmallows and vanilla. Spread the mixture evenly into the prepared pan. Press the reserved cookies and marshmallows into top of fudge.

3. Refrigerate for 2 hours or until firm. Remove fudge from pan and peel away foil. Cut into 16 squares. Cover with foil. Store in the refrigerator.

Makes: 2 pounds

Beverages

Tropical Champagne Ice

START TO FINISH: 5 hours 15 minutes

Prepping: 15 minutes
Freezing: 5 hours

- 3 bottles (16 fluid ounces **each**) V8 Splash® Tropical Blend Juice, chilled
- 1 bottle (750 ml) champagne (3 cups), chilled
- 1 teaspoon grated orange peel (optional)
- 4½ cups cut-up fresh fruit (mango, papaya **or** pineapple)

1. Stir the juice, champagne and orange peel, if desired, in a 13×9×2-inch metal baking pan.

2. Cover and freeze for 5 hours or until frozen. After 2 hours, stir with a fork every hour.

3. Scoop **about ½ cup** champagne ice into a stemmed glass or dessert dish. Top with the fruit. Serve immediately. Cover and freeze any leftover ice. Let it stand at room temperature for 5 minutes to soften before scooping.

Makes: 18 servings

Berry Rum Toddies

START TO FINISH: 10 minutes

Prepping/Cooking: 10 minutes

- 1 bottle (16 fluid ounces) V8 Splash® Berry Blend Juice (2 cups)
- 2 fluid ounces (¼ cup) dark spiced **or** regular rum
- ½ teaspoon ground cinnamon
- ¼ teaspoon ground ginger
- 2 cinnamon sticks

1. Heat the juice, rum, cinnamon and ginger in a 1-quart saucepan to a boil and cook for 5 minutes, stirring occasionally.

2. Pour the juice mixture into 2 mugs.

3. Serve with the cinnamon. Serve immediately.

Makes: 2 servings

Tropical Freeze

START TO FINISH: 10 minutes

Prepping: 10 minutes

- 1 bottle (16 fluid ounces) V8 Splash® Tropical Blend Juice (2 cups), chilled
- 1 pint orange **or** mango sherbet **or** vanilla ice cream
- 1 cup crushed ice
- 1 medium banana, sliced

1. Put the juice, sherbet, ice and banana in an electric blender container.
2. Cover and blend until it's smooth.
3. Serve immediately.

Makes: 4 servings

·87·
Beverages

Frosted Citrus Green Tea

START TO FINISH: 3 hours 30 minutes

Prepping: 2 hours
Freezing/Refrigerating: 1 hour 30 minutes

- 2 bottles (16 fluid ounces **each**) Diet V8 Splash® Tropical Blend Juice (4 cups), chilled
- 4 cups strong brewed green tea*
- Fresh mint sprigs (optional)
- Lemon slices (optional)

1. Pour **2 cups** juice into **1** ice cube tray. Freeze for 1 hour 30 minutes or until the mixture is frozen.

2. Mix the remaining juice and tea in an 8-cup measure. Refrigerate for at least 1 hour and 30 minutes.

3. Unmold the cubes from the tray and place 3 to 4 cubes in each of **6** tall glasses. Divide the tea mixture among the glasses. Serve with mint and lemon, if desired.

Makes: 6 servings

***Strong brewed tea:** Heat 4 cups of water in a 2-quart saucepan over high heat to a boil. Remove the pan from the heat. Add **8** tea bags and let them steep for 5 minutes. Remove the tea bags.

Lemon Sangria Punch

START TO FINISH: 10 minutes

Prepping: 10 minutes

- 1 bottle (64 fluid ounces) V8® 100% Vegetable Juice, chilled
- 1 container (64 fluid ounces) refrigerated lemonade
- 1 tablespoon Worcestershire sauce (optional)
- 2 lemons, thinly sliced
- 2 limes, thinly sliced
- 1 orange, thinly sliced
- Ice cubes

1. Stir the juice, lemonade and Worcestershire, if desired, lemons, limes and orange in an 8-quart punch bowl.

2. Serve immediately or refrigerate until serving time.

3. Pour over ice-filled tall glasses.

Makes: 20 servings

Bellini Splash

START TO FINISH: 5 minutes

Prepping: 5 minutes

- ½ cup **V8 Splash® Peach Lemonade or Mango Peach, chilled**
- ¼ cup **peach nectar, chilled**
- 1 cup **champagne, sparkling wine or sparkling cider, chilled**

1. Stir the juice and nectar in a 1-cup measure.
2. Divide between 2 fluted champagne glasses. Pour in champagne.
3. Serve immediately.

Makes: 2 servings

Cooking for a Crowd: Recipe may be doubled or tripled.

·91·
Beverages

Spicy Mary Martinis

START TO FINISH: 5 minutes

Prepping: 5 minutes

- 2 cans (5.5 fluid ounces **each**) V8® Spicy Hot Vegetable Juice
- 3 fluid ounces (6 tablespoons) pepper-flavored vodka
- Dash chipotle hot pepper sauce (or to taste)
- 2 cups ice cubes
- Seasoned salt (optional)
- 2 stalks celery

1. Put the juice, vodka, pepper sauce and ice in a cocktail shaker. Cover and shake until blended.

2. Strain into 2 chilled tall glasses rimmed with seasoned salt, if desired.

3. Serve with the celery.

Makes: 2 servings

Jump Start Smoothie

START TO FINISH: 10 minutes

Prepping: 10 minutes

- 1 bottle (16 fluid ounces) V8 Splash® Orange Pineapple Juice (2 cups), chilled
- 1 cup vanilla lowfat yogurt
- 2 cups frozen whole strawberries **or** raspberries

1. Put the juice, yogurt and strawberries in an electric blender container.
2. Cover and blend until smooth.
3. Serve immediately.

Makes: 4 servings

·93·
Beverages

Orange Mist

START TO FINISH: 5 minutes

Prepping: 5 minutes

- 1 bottle (46 fluid ounces) V8® 100% Vegetable Juice
- 1 can (6 ounces) frozen orange juice concentrate
- 1½ cups plain **or** orange-flavored seltzer water
- Ice cubes

1. Stir the vegetable juice and orange juice in a large pitcher until the mixture is smooth.
2. Add the seltzer water.
3. Pour over ice-filled tall glasses.

Makes: 10 servings

Index

Appetizers
Bloody Fingers 55
Goblin's Toes........................ 54
Italiano Fondue 2
Layered Pizza Dip 4
Porcupine Meatballs.............. 10
Single-Serve Southwest
    Dip Cups........................ 11
Spicy Grilled Quesadillas....... 8
Tex-Mex Toasts 7
Walnut-Cheddar Ball 6

Beef
Beef 'n' Bean Burritos........... 27
Beef Stroganoff 36
Chipotle Chili....................... 17
French Onion Burgers 22
Quick Ranchero Chili 30

Beef 'n' Bean Burritos................. 27
Beef Stroganoff............................ 36
Bellini Splash 91
Berry Rum Toddies 86

Beverages
Bellini Splash 91
Berry Rum Toddies 86
Frosted Citrus Green Tea 88
Jump Start Smoothie............. 93
Lemon Sangria Punch 90
Orange Mist 94
Spicy Mary Martinis 92
Tropical Champagne Ice 84
Tropical Freeze..................... 87

Bloody Fingers 55
Bourbon Orange Chocolate
   Lady Dessert 73
Broccoli & Noodles Supreme..... 64
Cheddar Broccoli Bake 56
Chicken Nacho Tacos................. 42
Chipotle Chili.............................. 17

Chocolate and Coconut
   Cream Fondue 70
Chocolate Cherry Ice
   Cream Cake 74
Crab and Asparagus Risotto 66
Cranberry Dijon Pork Chops...... 40
Creamy Citrus Tomato Soup
   with Pesto Croutons 12

Desserts
Bourbon Orange Chocolate
    Lady Dessert.................... 73
Chocolate and Coconut
    Cream Fondue................. 70
Chocolate Cherry Ice
    Cream Cake 74
Fishy Families 68
I'm Dreamy for White
    Chocolate Fondue........... 72
Mini Chocolate Cookie
    Cheesecakes 76
Quick & Easy Berry
    Shortcakes....................... 80
Southern Pecan Crisps........... 78
Super Chunky Fudge 82

Fish and Seafood
Crab and Asparagus
    Risotto 66
Italian Fish Fillets 28

Fishy Families 68
French Onion Burgers................. 22
Frosted Citrus Green Tea 88
Glazed Snow Peas and
   Carrots 58
Goblin's Toes 54
Green Bean Casserole 44
Grilled Pork in Pitas 24
Hearty Bean & Barley Soup 16
Heavenly Sweet Potatoes........... 50
Herb Roasted Turkey.................. 48
Holiday Potato Pancakes............ 46
I'm Dreamy for White
   Chocolate Fondue................ 72
Italian Fish Fillets 28

Italiano Fondue 2
Jump Start Smoothie 93
Layered Cranberry Walnut
 Stuffing 51
Layered Pizza Dip 4
Lemon Sangria Punch 90
Mediterranean Chop Salad 59
Mini Chocolate Cookie
 Cheesecakes 76
Mozzarella Zucchini Skillet 65
Orange Mist 94
Porcupine Meatballs 10

Pork

Cranberry Dijon Pork
 Chops 40
Grilled Pork in Pitas 24

Potato Crusted Chicken 34

Poultry

Bloody Fingers 55
Chicken Nacho Tacos 42
Herb Roasted Turkey 48
Porcupine Meatballs 10
Potato Crusted Chicken 34
Quick Chicken Parmesan 31
Ranchero Oven-Fried
 Chicken 38
Southwest Salsa Chicken
 with Fresh Greens 26
Spaghetti Soup 20
Spicy Grilled Quesadillas 8
Tomato-Basil Chicken 32

Quick & Easy Berry Shortcakes ... 80
Quick Chicken Parmesan 31
Quick Ranchero Chili 30
Ranchero Oven-Fried Chicken 38
Roasted Tomato & Barley Soup ... 14

Salads and Sides

Broccoli & Noodles
 Supreme 64
Cheddar Broccoli Bake 56

Crab and Asparagus
 Risotto 66
Glazed Snow Peas and
 Carrots 58
Green Bean Casserole 44
Heavenly Sweet Potatoes 50
Holiday Potato Pancakes 46
Layered Cranberry Walnut
 Stuffing 51
Mediterranean Chop Salad ... 59
Mozzarella Zucchini Skillet ... 65
Spaghetti Squash Alfredo 62
Swiss Vegetable Bake 52
Toasted Corn & Sage
 Harvest Risotto 60

Single-Serve Southwest
 Dip Cups 11

Soups and Stews

Creamy Citrus Tomato Soup
 with Pesto Croutons 12
Hearty Bean & Barley Soup ... 16
Roasted Tomato & Barley
 Soup 14
Spaghetti Soup 20
White Bean with Fennel
 Soup 18

Southern Pecan Crisps 78
Southwest Salsa Chicken with
 Fresh Greens 26
Spaghetti Soup 20
Spaghetti Squash Alfredo 62
Spicy Grilled Quesadillas 8
Spicy Mary Martinis 92
Super Chunky Fudge 82
Swiss Vegetable Bake 52
Tex-Mex Toasts 7
Toasted Corn & Sage Harvest
 Risotto 60
Tomato-Basil Chicken 32
Tropical Champagne Ice 84
Tropical Freeze 87
Walnut-Cheddar Ball 6
White Bean with Fennel Soup 18